United States Presidents

John Quincy Adams

Paul Joseph
ABDO Publishing Company

visit us at
www.abdopub.com

Published by Abdo Publishing Company 4940 Viking Drive, Edina, Minnesota 55435.
Copyright © 1999 by Abdo Consulting Group, Inc. International copyrights reserved in
all countries. No part of this book may be reproduced in any form without written
permission from the publisher.

Printed in the United States.

Cover and Interior Photo credits: AP/Wide World, Archive, Corbis-Bettmann

Contributing editors: Robert Italia, Tamara L. Britton, K. M. Brielmaier
Book design/maps: Patrick Laurel

Library of Congress Cataloging-in-Publication Data

Joseph, Paul, 1970-
    John Quincy Adams / Paul Joseph.
        p. cm. -- (United States presidents)
    Includes index.
    Summary: A biography of the man who served as foreign minister,
senator, and sixth president of the United States.
    ISBN 1-57765-231-2
    1. Adams, John Quincy, 1767-1848--Juvenile literature.
2. Presidents--United States--Biography--Juvenile literature.
[1. Adams, John Quincy, 1767-1848. 2. Presidents.] I. Title.
II. Series: United States presidents (Edina, Minn.)
E377.J67   1999
973.5'5'092--dc21
    [B]   98-12976
                                                       CIP
                                                       AC

Revised Edition 2002

Contents

John Quincy Adams

*J*ohn Quincy Adams was the sixth president of the United States. His father, John Adams, was the second U.S. president.

John Quincy grew up during the **American Revolution**. As a child, he saw many battles. He also traveled to Europe with his father. He attended school in France.

As a young man, John Quincy Adams was a lawyer. He also was a writer and a **diplomat**. Later, Adams was elected to the U.S. Senate. And he served as **secretary of state**.

President Adams fought for what he thought was right. But he also made political enemies. They kept Adams from succeeding.

After he was president, Adams served 17 years in the **House of Representatives**. There, he fought the spread of slavery in the United States.

Throughout his adult life, John Quincy Adams served his country. His work helped change the nation.

John Quincy Adams

John Quincy Adams (1767-1848)
Sixth President

BORN:	July 11, 1767
PLACE OF BIRTH:	Braintree (Quincy), Massachusetts
ANCESTRY:	English
FATHER:	John Adams (1735-1826)
MOTHER:	Abigail Smith Adams (1744-1818)
WIFE:	Louisa Catherine Johnson (1775-1852)
CHILDREN:	Four: 3 boys, 1 girl
EDUCATION:	Studied in Paris, Amsterdam, Leiden, and The Hague; Harvard College; studied law (1788-1790) with Theophilus Parsons
RELIGION:	Unitarian
OCCUPATION:	Lawyer, professor, writer, diplomat
MILITARY SERVICE:	None
POLITICAL PARTY:	Federalist 1808; Democratic-Republican to 1825; National Republican thereafter

OFFICES HELD:	Minister to the Netherlands; minister to Prussia; member of Massachusetts Senate; U.S. senator; minister to Russia; minister to Great Britain; secretary of state; member of U.S. House of Representatives
AGE AT INAUGURATION:	57
YEARS SERVED:	1825-1829
VICE PRESIDENT:	John C. Calhoun
DIED:	February 23, 1848, Washington, D.C., age 80
CAUSE OF DEATH:	Stroke

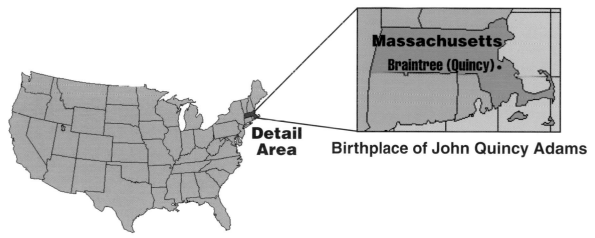

Massachusetts
Braintree (Quincy)
Detail Area
Birthplace of John Quincy Adams

Starting Early

*J*ohn Quincy Adams was born July 11, 1767, in Braintree, Massachusetts. The town was later renamed Quincy. He was the oldest son of John and Abigail Adams. John Quincy had an older sister and three younger brothers.

Young John Quincy saw U.S. history being made. He and his mother watched the Battle of Bunker Hill near the family farm. It was the first major battle of the **American Revolution**.

John Quincy and his father saw British soldiers in the streets in Boston, Massachusetts. His father told him about the Boston Massacre, when colonists were shot during a fight. And he learned about the Boston Tea Party, when colonists protested a tea tax.

In 1778, John Adams went to Europe as a **diplomat**. John Quincy joined him. He lived there for most of his teen years. He learned Latin, Greek, French, and Dutch.

When he was 14, John Quincy went to Russia with Francis Dana. Dana was a U.S. **envoy**. John Quincy worked as his assistant. A year later, John Quincy joined his father in Paris, France. He helped his father with the treaty that ended the **American Revolution**.

In 1785, John Quincy returned to America. He attended Harvard College in Cambridge, Massachusetts. He became a good speaker and musician. John Quincy graduated in just two years.

John Quincy Adams decided to work for a law office. In three years, he became a lawyer. Adams also wrote political newspaper articles. President George Washington liked Adams's writing. He made Adams minister to the Netherlands.

Young John Quincy Adams

Europe

*I*n 1794, John Quincy Adams sailed to Europe. He reported to George Washington on events in the Netherlands and other European countries.

On a trip to London, England, Adams met Louisa Catherine Johnson. Louisa was born in London in 1775. John Quincy and Louisa were married on July 26, 1797. Louisa is the only first lady born outside of the United States.

Adams became minister to Prussia in 1797. He and Louisa moved to Berlin. There, Adams helped write a treaty. He also traveled with his wife through Europe.

John Quincy and Louisa's first child, George Washington Adams, was born in Berlin in 1801. He was named after President Washington. That year, Adams and his family returned to Boston. Adams worked as a lawyer.

Opposite page:
Louisa Adams

Senator Adams

*J*ohn Quincy Adams decided to work in politics. In 1802, he was elected to the Massachusetts Senate. In 1803, Adams won election to the U.S. Senate.

In 1807, President Thomas Jefferson called for a shipping **embargo**. Adams supported the president. This action made Adams unpopular in the New England states. They depended on shipping to make money. The next year, Adams quit the Senate before he could be replaced. He returned home to practice law.

John Quincy and Louisa had two more sons. John was born in 1803. Charles Francis was born in 1807. A daughter, Louisa Catherine, was born in 1811. But she died the next year.

In 1809, President James Madison made Adams minister to Russia. There, Adams saw the emperor of France, Napoleon Bonaparte, invade the country.

Napoleon Bonaparte

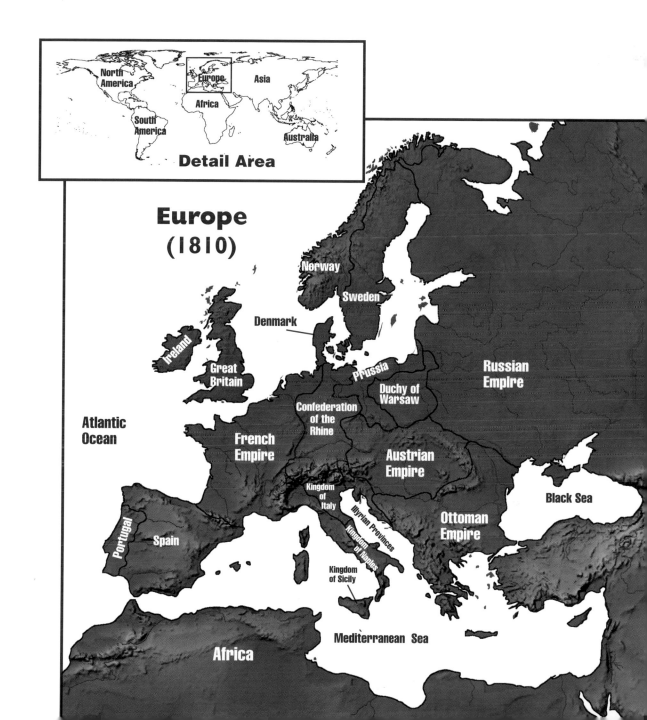

Detail Area

North America

South America

Europe

Africa

Asia

Australia

Europe
(1810)

Norway

Sweden

Denmark

Ireland

Great Britain

Prussia

Duchy of Warsaw

Russian Empire

Atlantic Ocean

Confederation of the Rhine

French Empire

Austrian Empire

Black Sea

Kingdom of Italy

Illyrian Provinces

Ottoman Empire

Portugal

Spain

Kingdom of Naples

Kingdom of Sicily

Mediterranean Sea

Africa

The Making of the Sixth United States President

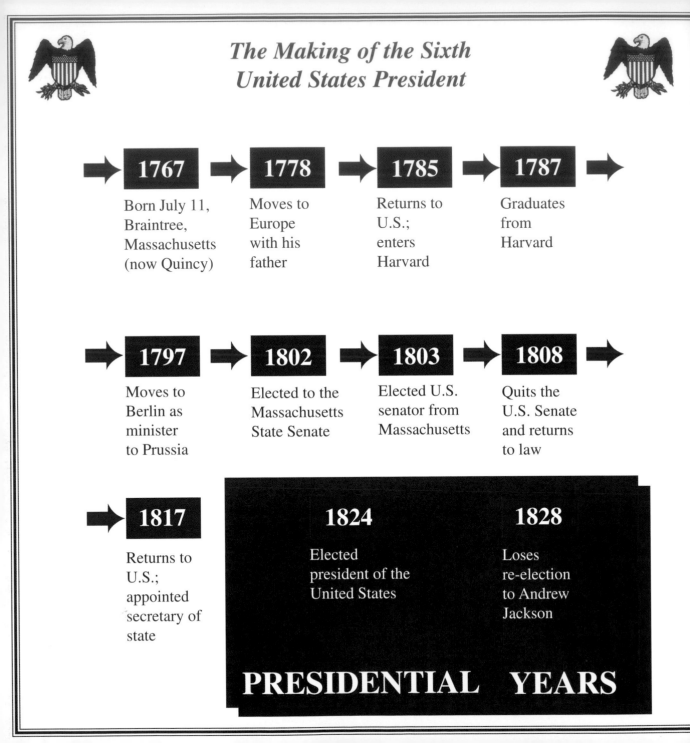

1767 → Born July 11, Braintree, Massachusetts (now Quincy)

1778 → Moves to Europe with his father

1785 → Returns to U.S.; enters Harvard

1787 → Graduates from Harvard

1797 → Moves to Berlin as minister to Prussia

1802 → Elected to the Massachusetts State Senate

1803 → Elected U.S. senator from Massachusetts

1808 → Quits the U.S. Senate and returns to law

1817 → Returns to U.S.; appointed secretary of state

1824 Elected president of the United States

1828 Loses re-election to Andrew Jackson

PRESIDENTIAL YEARS

John Quincy Adams

"No person could be degraded by serving the people as a representative. . . . Nor, in my opinion, would an ex-president . . . be degraded by serving as a selectman . . . if elected thereto by the people."

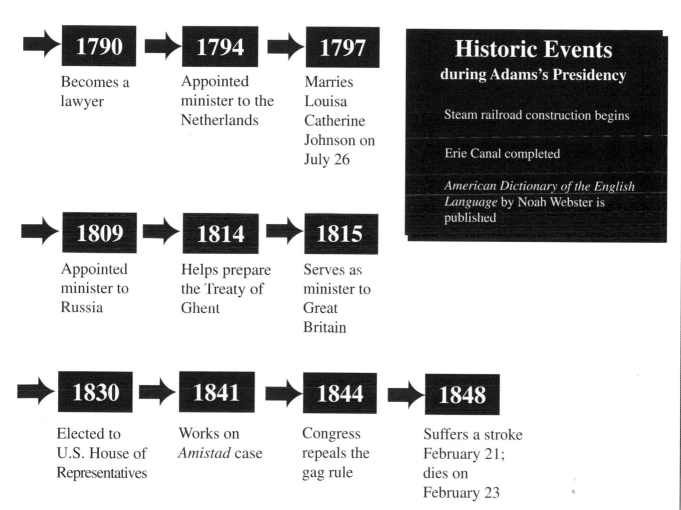

1790
Becomes a lawyer

1794
Appointed minister to the Netherlands

1797
Marries Louisa Catherine Johnson on July 26

Historic Events
during Adams's Presidency

Steam railroad construction begins

Erie Canal completed

American Dictionary of the English Language by Noah Webster is published

1809
Appointed minister to Russia

1814
Helps prepare the Treaty of Ghent

1815
Serves as minister to Great Britain

1830
Elected to U.S. House of Representatives

1841
Works on *Amistad* case

1844
Congress repeals the gag rule

1848
Suffers a stroke February 21; dies on February 23

Secretary Adams

*I*n 1811, President Madison wanted Adams to join the U.S. Supreme Court. Adams felt honored. But he turned down the offer. He stayed in Europe to work for peace.

America and Britain fought each other in the **War of 1812**. In 1814, Adams and a group of Americans went to Ghent, Belgium. They wanted to make peace with the British. Four months later, the Peace Treaty of Ghent was signed.

Adams served as minister to Great Britain from 1815 to 1817. He and his family lived quietly in a country house near London, England.

In 1817, Adams returned to the United States. President Monroe made him **secretary of state**. At that time, Spain owned the Florida Territory. When America invaded Florida, Adams helped bring peace. He made a deal with Spanish leaders that gave Florida to the United States.

The United States
(1817-1825)

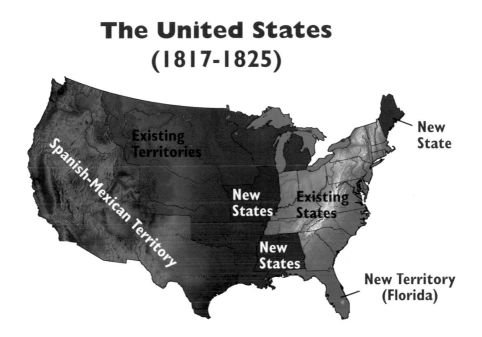

Existing
Territories

Spanish-Mexican Territory

New
States

New
States

Existing
States

New
State

New Territory
(Florida)

Adams also helped write the Monroe Doctrine. It said that the U.S. would not allow Europe to attack countries in North and South America. Many historians consider Adams the finest **secretary of state** in American history.

The Sixth President

Adams did well as **secretary of state**. So, he decided to run for president in 1824.

Adams was one of five candidates. But **Secretary of War** John C. Calhoun withdrew from the contest. He ran for vice president. That left **Secretary of the Treasury** William H. Crawford, **Speaker of the House** Henry Clay, and General Andrew Jackson.

Each candidate had support from parts of the country. When the **electoral college** votes were counted, Jackson had 99, Adams 84, Crawford 41, and Clay 37. To win, a candidate had to have more than half the total votes.

A portrait of John Quincy Adams

According to the U.S. Constitution, the U.S. **House of Representatives** now had to choose the president. Voting by state, they chose among the top three candidates. That meant Henry Clay was out of the race.

Clay decided to back Adams. Clay's supporters voted for Adams. Adams received most of the votes. He became the sixth president of the United States.

Adams wanted the best people for his **cabinet**. He refused to choose people just because they belonged to a certain political party.

Adams asked Andrew Jackson to be **secretary of war**. But Jackson refused. So, Adams picked Henry Barbour instead. Adams chose Henry Clay to be **secretary of state**.

Jackson's supporters in **Congress** protested. Clay had helped Adams's election. They claimed that Adams and Clay had made a deal so they could get into office. Now, Adams had political enemies in Congress.

The Seven "Hats" of the U.S. President

A president can serve only two terms. Each term lasts four years. When Adams was president, this law did not exist.

A president is elected or re-elected every four years.

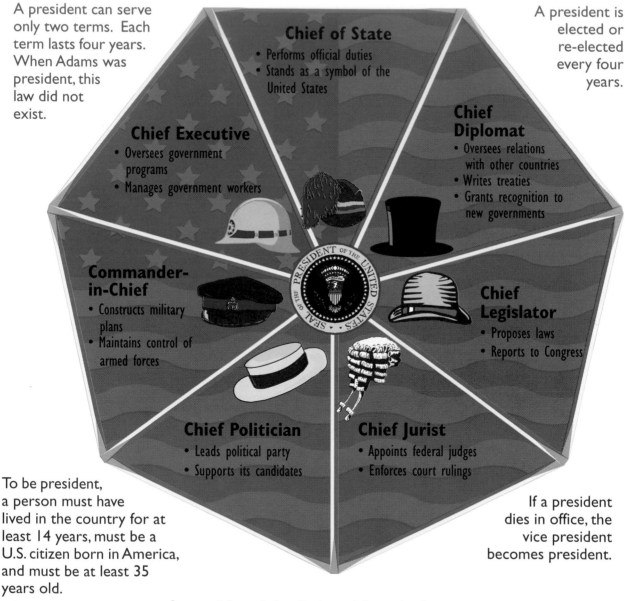

Chief of State
- Performs official duties
- Stands as a symbol of the United States

Chief Executive
- Oversees government programs
- Manages government workers

Chief Diplomat
- Oversees relations with other countries
- Writes treaties
- Grants recognition to new governments

Commander-in-Chief
- Constructs military plans
- Maintains control of armed forces

Chief Legislator
- Proposes laws
- Reports to Congress

Chief Politician
- Leads political party
- Supports its candidates

Chief Jurist
- Appoints federal judges
- Enforces court rulings

To be president, a person must have lived in the country for at least 14 years, must be a U.S. citizen born in America, and must be at least 35 years old.

If a president dies in office, the vice president becomes president.

As president, John Quincy Adams had seven jobs.

The Three Branches of the U.S. Government

Congress is in the Capitol Building in Washington, D.C. It can pass laws and stop the president's veto. Congress also can change the Constitution to stop the president's plans or Supreme Court rulings.

The president lives in the White House in Washington, D.C. He or she can stop (veto) laws passed by Congress, and propose new laws. The president also can choose Supreme Court judges.

The Supreme Court is in the Supreme Court Building in Washington, D.C. It can stop laws passed by Congress. It also can change or stop the president's plans.

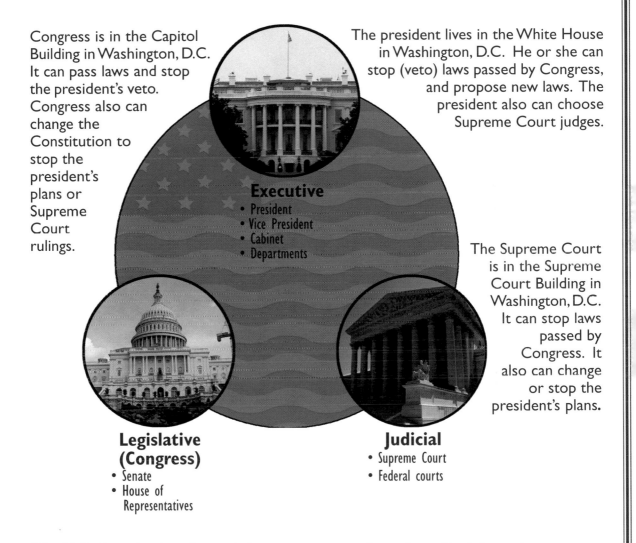

Executive
- President
- Vice President
- Cabinet
- Departments

Legislative (Congress)
- Senate
- House of Representatives

Judicial
- Supreme Court
- Federal courts

The U.S. Constitution formed three government branches. Each branch has power over the others. So, no single group or person can control the country. The Constitution calls this "separation of powers."

Running the Country

*P*resident Adams wanted many things for America. He wanted to stop slavery. He wanted to connect America with new roads and canals. Adams also wanted money to help farmers. And he wanted to build new factories and create new jobs.

Adams proposed building many public universities. And he wanted new laws to protect Native Americans. But Adams still had many political enemies. **Congress** voted down everything he wanted.

Adams was sad about his battles with Congress. He became upset. He had trouble eating and sleeping. And he lost weight.

Adams kept busy by taking long walks, swimming, and reading. He also wrote in his diary. Adams held little hope for re-election in 1828.

The United States during Adams's Presidency (1825-1829)

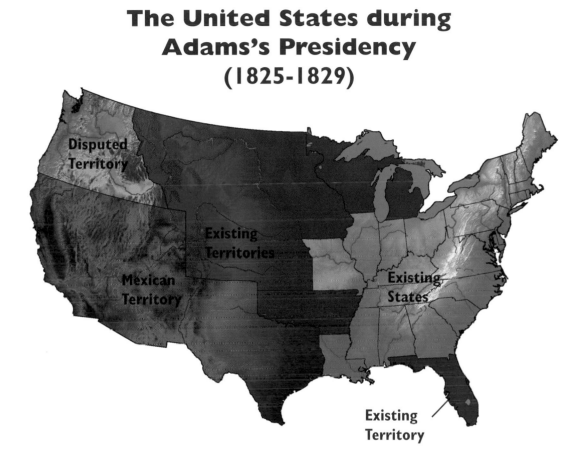

Disputed Territory

Existing Territories

Mexican Territory

Existing States

Existing Territory

The Election of 1828

*I*n 1828, Adams entered one of the ugliest elections in U.S. history.

President Adams's foe was Andrew Jackson. Adams's vice president, John Calhoun, disliked Adams's ideas. He decided to run as Jackson's vice president. Adams chose Richard Rush.

The campaign was hateful. Jackson was called stupid and foolish. Adams was called dishonest. Adams had too many political enemies to win the election. Andrew Jackson became president.

Adams took his election defeat very hard. He refused to attend Jackson's **inauguration**. But soon, Adams was glad his four years as president were over. In 1829, Adams returned to Braintree, Massachusetts.

Opposite page:
The home of
John Quincy Adams

Old Man Eloquent

*J*ohn Quincy Adams was unsure about his future. But in 1830, he was elected to the **House of Representatives**. He is the only president in U.S. history to be elected to political office after being president.

Adams had not been a popular president. But he was a popular representative. Many congressmen admired the great knowledge he showed in his speeches. They called him Old Man Eloquent.

In 1841, Adams worked on an important law case. A group of captured Africans were on the slave ship *Amistad*. The Africans took control of the ship near Cuba. They sailed to the United States, but were arrested. Adams became their lawyer. He fought for and won their freedom in court. The Africans returned home to Africa.

In **Congress**, Adams continued to fight slavery. Congressmen from the South had passed a "gag rule." No one could talk about slavery in Congress. This kept laws against slavery from being passed. Adams fought this rule for eight years. Congress ended the gag rule in 1844.

On February 21, 1848, Adams suffered a stroke in the **House of Representatives**. He died February 23.

John Quincy Adams had earned the nation's respect. As **secretary of state**, he helped America's troubles with other countries. As president and congressman, he will always be remembered for his fight against slavery.

Adams suffered a stroke in Congress.

Fun Facts

- John Quincy Adams was the only president whose father was a president. Adams lived in Europe the entire time his father was president.

- Adams woke up at 4:00 or 5:00 each morning. The first thing he would do was write in his diary.

- On warm mornings, Adams swam in the Potomac River. One day, a female reporter surprised him. She sat on his clothes and refused to go away until he gave her an interview.

- Adams was the only president who was a published poet.

- Adams loved to play pool. He bought a pool table for the White House. Most Americans were not happy about this purchase. So, Adams paid for it with his own money.

- Adams lived long enough to see the camera invented. Toward the end of his life, he had his picture taken. John Quincy Adams is the first president of whom a photograph exists.

One of three known photographs of John Quincy Adams

Glossary

American Revolution - a war fought from 1775 to 1783 between Great Britain and its American colonies. The Americans won their independence and created the United States.

cabinet - a group of advisers chosen by the president.

Congress - the lawmaking group of a state or country. It is made up of the Senate and the House of Representatives.

diplomat - a person who deals with representatives of other countries.

electoral college - the group that formally elects the president and vice president. When people vote for president, the political party—Republican, Democratic, or other—that gets the most votes in each state sends its representatives to the electoral college. There, they vote for their party's candidate.

embargo - when a country is stopped from trading with other countries.

envoy - a representative of a country who is sent to another country.

House of Representatives - a group of people elected by citizens to represent them. They meet in Washington, D.C., and make laws for the entire country.

inauguration - when a person is sworn into office.

secretary of state - a member of the president's cabinet who handles problems with other countries.

secretary of the treasury - a member of the president's cabinet who handles economic policy.

secretary of war - a member of the president's cabinet who handles the nation's defense.

speaker of the house - the leader of the majority party of the House who runs House sessions.

War of 1812 - a war fought from 1812 to 1814 against Great Britain over shipping and the capture of U.S. sailors.

Internet Sites

PBS American Presidents Series
http://www.americanpresidents.org
Visit the PBS Web site which features the biographies of each president. Check out the key events of each presidency, speeches, fun facts, and trivia games.

Welcome to the White House
http://www.whitehouse.gov
The official Web site of the White House. After an introduction from the current president of the United States, the site takes you through biographies of each president. Get information on White House history, art in the White House, first ladies, first families, and much more.

POTUS—Presidents of the United States
http://www.ipl.org/ref/POTUS/
In this Web site you will find background information, election results, cabinet members, presidency highlights, and some odd facts on each of the presidents. Links to biographies, historical documents, audio and video files, and other presidential sites are also included to enrich this site.

These sites are subject to change. Go to your favorite search engine and type in United States presidents for more sites.

Pass It On

   History enthusiasts: educate readers around the country by passing on information you've learned about presidents or other important people who have changed history. Share your little-known facts and interesting stories. We want to hear from you!

To get posted on the ABDO Publishing Company Web site, email us at "History@abdopub.com"
Visit the ABDO Publishing Company Web site at www.abdopub.com

Index